AFRICAN AMERICAN LEADERS OF COURAGE

FREDERICK DOUGLASS

KRISTEN SUSIENKA

PowerKiDS
press™

New York

Published in 2020 by The Rosen Publishing Group, Inc.
29 East 21st Street, New York, NY 10010

First Edition

Editor: Kristen Susienka
Book Design: Michael Flynn

Photo Credits: Cover, pp. 1, 17 Bettmann/Getty Images; series background Kharchenko Ruslan/Shutterstock.com; p. 5 Everett Historical/Shutterstock.com; p. 7 (map) pingebat/Shutterstock.com; p. 7 (paper texture) Color Symphony/Shutterstock.com; p. 7 (tobacco field) Robert Donovan/Shutterstock.com; p. 9 Smith Collection/Goda/Archive Photos/Getty Images; p. 11 The Picture Art Collection/Alamy; p. 13 courtesy of Library of Congress; p. 15 Hulton Archive/Getty Images; p. 19 (main image) Smith Collection/Gado/Archive Photos/Getty Images; p. 19 (inset) https://en.wikipedia.org/wiki/File:NorthStarfrontpage.jpg; p. 21 Drew Angerer/Getty Images.

Library of Congress Cataloging-in-Publication Data

Names: Susienka, Kristen, author.
Title: Frederick Douglass / Kristen Susienka.
Description: New York : PowerKids Press, [2020] | Series: African American
  leaders of courage | Includes index.
Identifiers: LCCN 2019008803| ISBN 9781725308343 (pbk.) | ISBN 9781725308367
  (library bound) | ISBN 9781725308350 (6 pack)
Subjects: LCSH: Douglass, Frederick, 1818-1895–Juvenile literature. |
  Slaves–United States–Biography–Juvenile literature. |
  Abolitionists–United States–Biography–Juvenile literature. | African
  American abolitionists–Biography–Juvenile literature. | Antislavery
  movements–United States–History–Juvenile literature. | African
  Americans–History–19th century–Juvenile literature.
Classification: LCC E449.D75 S97 2020 | DDC 973.8092 [B] –dc23
LC record available at https://lccn.loc.gov/2019008803

Manufactured in the United States of America

CPSIA Compliance Information: Batch #CWPK20. For Further Information contact Rosen Publishing, New York, New York at 1-800-237-9932.

CONTENTS

An Important Man

American history has many famous people. Frederick Douglass is one of the most famous. He was born a **slave** in the early 1800s. As an adult, he escaped to **freedom**. Once free, he wrote books, gave speeches, and helped other slaves become free.

5

A Boy with No Birthday

Frederick Douglass didn't know his birthday. He thought he was born in 1818. He grew up in the state of Maryland. Frederick worked on a **plantation**. He didn't live with his parents. Instead, he lived with his grandma and other slaves.

UNITED STATES OF AMERICA

Maryland

Life as a Slave

When Frederick was eight years old, he went to live with the Auld family. Mr. and Mrs. Auld lived in a house in Baltimore, Maryland. Frederick worked for them as a slave. Mrs. Auld taught Frederick the alphabet, even though she wasn't supposed to.

**Baltimore, Maryland
1802**

9

The Trouble with Learning

Mr. Auld didn't want his wife to teach Frederick. Slaves weren't supposed to learn to read or write. She stopped teaching him. Frederick didn't stop learning, though. He taught himself how to read and write. But he never let the Aulds know.

Runaway

When Frederick was 16, he was sent to another plantation. The owner and others beat him. In 1838, Frederick escaped. He wanted to be free. Some of his friends helped him. He went to New York City and then Massachusetts.

Finding Freedom

Frederick started a new life in Massachusetts. He had to be careful. He didn't want his former owner to find him. He changed his last name. His **original** last name was Bailey. When he was free, he chose the last name Douglass.

15

Speaking About Slavery

In 1841, Frederick Douglass started to speak about his life as a slave. Many people wanted to know what it was like. Frederick was a great speaker. People believed his words. In 1845, he wrote his first **autobiography**.

Getting the Word Out

From 1845 to 1847, Frederick visited Ireland, Scotland, and England. He talked about slavery there. People in England bought his freedom. When he went home, Frederick moved to Rochester, New York. There, he started a newspaper called *The North Star*.

front page of
The North Star

19

Frederick's Lasting Mark

Frederick Douglass continued to work to end slavery. He fought for rights for African Americans and women. He died in 1895, but many people remember him for his bravery, his speeches, and his writings. He believed all people should be free.

THE LIFE OF FREDERICK DOUGLASS

1818 — Frederick Douglass is born.

1838 — Frederick escapes to freedom.

1841 — Frederick gives his first speech.

1845 — Frederick writes his first autobiography.

1895 — Frederick dies.

GLOSSARY

autobiography: A book that tells the story of a person's life that is written by the person it is about.

freedom: The state of being free.

original: Happening or existing first.

plantation: A large farm.

slave: A person "owned" by another person and forced to work without pay.

INDEX

WEBSITES

Due to the changing nature of Internet links, PowerKids Press has developed an online list of websites related to the subject of this book. This site is updated regularly. Please use this link to access the list: www.powerkidslinks.com/AALC/douglass